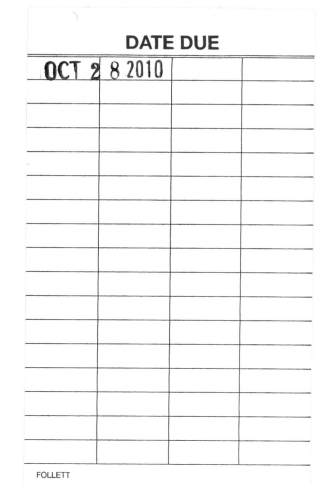

DATE DUE

OCT 2 8 2010			

FOLLETT

It is springtime. Two beekeepers have placed a beehive on a hill.

Activity begins around the hive. The honeybees and the beekeepers are…

THE HONEY MAKERS

GAIL GIBBONS

MORROW JUNIOR BOOKS
NEW YORK

Watercolors, colored pencils, and black pen were used for the full-color illustrations. The text type is 16-point Souvenir.

Manufactured in China.

10

Library of Congress Cataloging-in-Publication Data
Gibbons, Gail.
The honey makers/by Gail Gibbons.
p.   cm.
Summary: Covers the physical structure of honeybees and how they live in colonies, as well as how they produce honey and are managed by beekeepers.
ISBN 0-688-11386-9 (trade) — ISBN 0-688-11387-7 (library)
— ISBN 0-688-17531-7 (pbk.)
1. Honeybee—Juvenile literature.   2. Bee culture—Juvenile literature.   3. Honey—Juvenile literature   [1. Honeybee.   2. Bees.   3. Bee culture.   4. Honey.]   I. Title.
QL568.A6G5   1996   595.79'9—dc20   95-42053   CIP   AC

Special thanks to Dr. Gordon R. Nielsen, entomologist, Hinesburg, Vermont.

Thanks also to Keith and Delta Merchand of Smutty Hollow Bee Supplies, Monroe, New Hampshire.

HONEYBEE

COLONY

Hummm…Honeybees travel to and from the hive. Their earliest ancestors lived about 80 million years ago. The scientific name for *honeybee* comes from the Latin words *Apis mellifera,* meaning "honey bearer." Honeybees are social creatures. They form highly structured groups called *colonies.* In a colony, as many as 50,000 or more bees live together and work at their own special jobs.

WILD
HONEYBEE
HIVE

WOODEN
BEEHIVE

Many honeybees like to make their homes in dark, enclosed places. Often a colony of wild honeybees builds its hive in a hollow tree. Honeybees cared for by today's beekeepers live in box-shaped wooden hives.

CELL

HONEY

Inside the beehive, the honeybees are building an amazing structure called a *honeycomb.* It is made up of countless six-sided cells. Stored in many of these wax cells is the food that bees and people love to eat...honey!

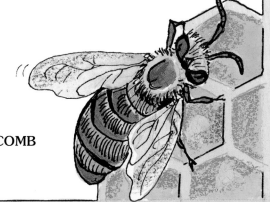

HONEYCOMB

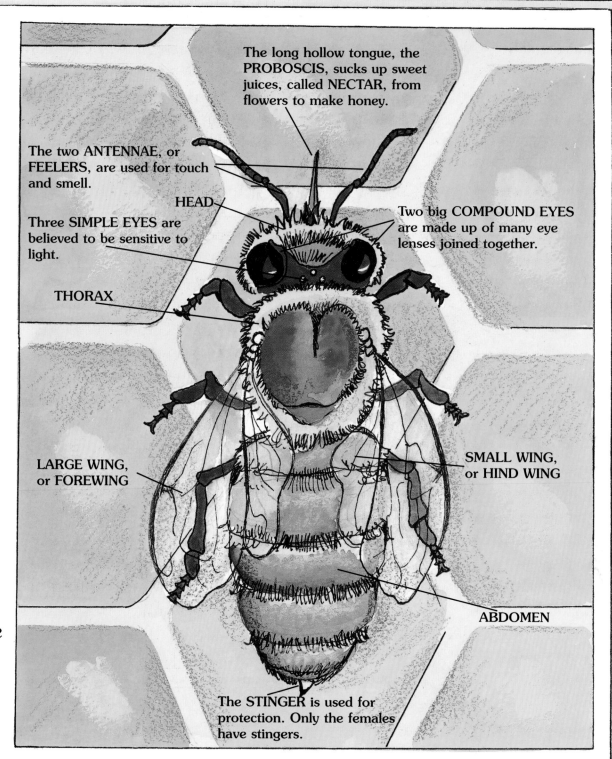

WORKER BEE

DRONE BEE

QUEEN BEE

The long hollow tongue, the PROBOSCIS, sucks up sweet juices, called NECTAR, from flowers to make honey.

The two ANTENNAE, or FEELERS, are used for touch and smell.

HEAD

Two big COMPOUND EYES are made up of many eye lenses joined together.

Three SIMPLE EYES are believed to be sensitive to light.

THORAX

LARGE WING, or FOREWING

SMALL WING, or HIND WING

ABDOMEN

The STINGER is used for protection. Only the females have stingers.

Three different kinds of honeybees live inside all beehives. There is one *queen,* about 100 male *drones,* and thousands of female *worker bees.* Like all insects, bees have three body parts. There is the *head,* the *thorax,* and the *abdomen.* Honeybees have other parts, too.

DRONE BEE

QUEEN BEE

The *queen* is the largest of the honeybees, and she can live the longest—from three to five years. All the other bees in the colony live for about two months, except over winter, when they live a few months longer. It is the queen's job to make sure the hive never runs out of bees. To do this, she leaves the hive to mate with her drones. Then she lays as many as 2,000 eggs a day! *Drones* are usually smaller than the queen; their only job is to mate with her.

Most cells in the beehive are used for storing honey, but some are used for the queen to lay her eggs. These are called *brood cells*. In each brood cell, a bee will develop and grow. The largest brood cells are *queen brood cells*, also called *royal cells*. *Drone brood cells* are smaller. Even smaller are the *worker brood cells*. The eggs in those cells will become worker bees. Although all worker bees are female, they do not lay eggs. Instead, they do the work of the beehive.

WORKER BEE

WORKER BROOD CELL

QUEEN BROOD CELL, or ROYAL CELL

DRONE BROOD CELL

LARVA

WORKER BEE called a NURSE BEE

BEEMILK is a milky syrup that is full of nutrition. It is made by glands inside the nurse worker bee.

BEEBREAD is a combination of pollen and honey.

ROYAL JELLY is made the same way as beemilk, but it is more nutritious.

QUEEN LARVA

Most eggs the queen lays are no bigger than the period at the end of this sentence. After three days a *larva* hatches from each one. For the next three days worker bees called *nurse bees* feed the larva *beemilk*. Then they feed it *beebread*. A queen larva is fed *royal jelly* throughout its growth.

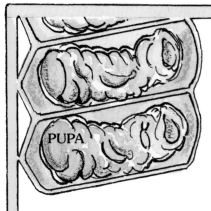

PUPA

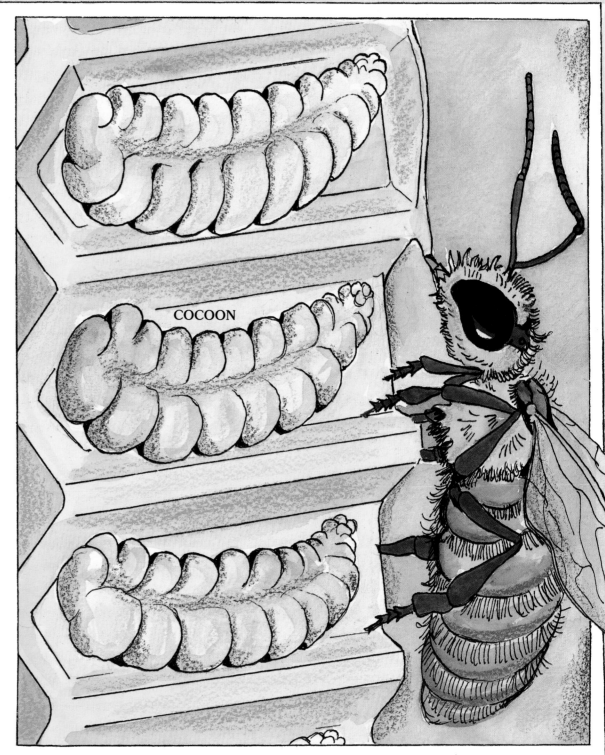

COCOON

Each larva grows quickly, then spins a silky *cocoon* around itself. Inside the cocoon, a *pupa* develops. A nurse bee seals the cell with wax.

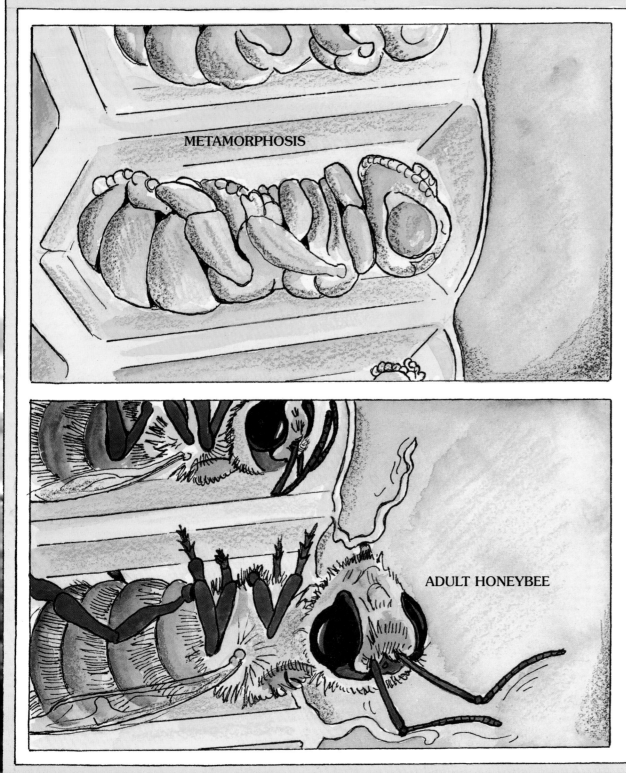

METAMORPHOSIS

Little by little, the pupa changes. It begins to look more like an adult insect. This process is called *metamorphosis*. Queens develop in about 16 days from the time the eggs are laid. The metamorphosis of drones and workers takes about 21 to 24 days. Finally, after the transformation is complete, an adult bee chews its way out of the brood cell…an adult honeybee.

ADULT HONEYBEE

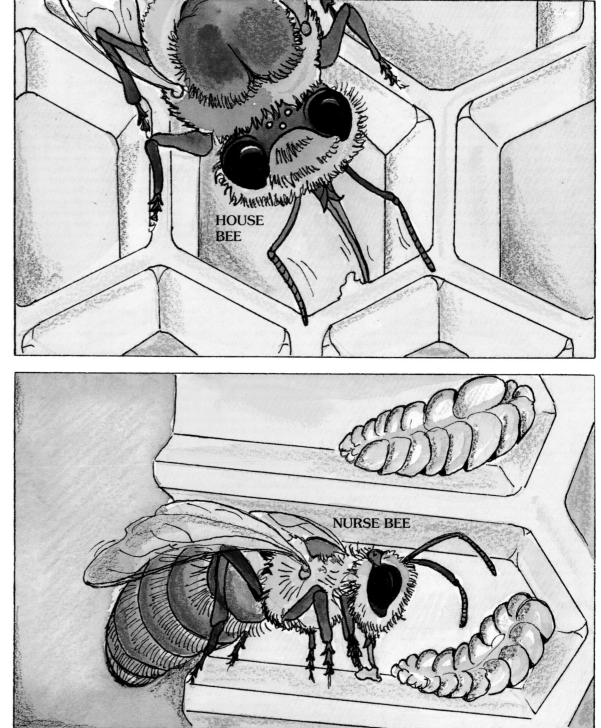

HOUSE
BEE

NURSE BEE

This honeybee is a worker bee. From the minute she comes out of her brood cell she is "as busy as a bee." For the next three weeks she will have a number of different jobs to do inside the hive. First she is a *house bee*, cleaning and polishing the cells. About three days later she becomes a *nurse bee*.

WAX-MAKING BEE

COURT

After ten days of being a nurse bee she becomes a *wax-making bee*. She makes flakes of wax in her abdomen and chews them to mold new cells or repair old ones. Wax-making bees are also in charge of storing the nectar and pollen that other honeybees bring back to the hive. Other workers care for the queen. They are her *court*. They cluster around the queen to continually feed and groom her.

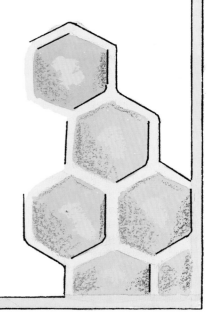

STINGER

GUARD BEE

About a week later the wax-making bee becomes a *guard bee* and begins its outdoor life. Guard bees protect the hive. They chase away intruders with their *stingers.* They also alert the other bees by spreading a special scent when there is danger. A guard bee will sometimes die in battle to protect the hive and its honey.

The worker bee is now about three weeks old. She is ready to become a *forager bee,* her last job, but a very important one. Forager bees are the bees you see zipping from flower to flower. They collect sweet juices, called *nectar,* from the flowers for honey making.

FORAGER BEE

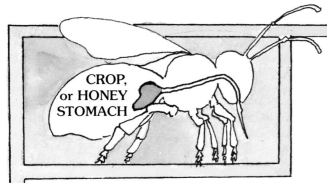

CROP,
or HONEY
STOMACH

PROBOSCIS

POLLEN BASKET

At each flower the forager bee collects nectar with her *proboscis.* She stores the nectar in a special part of her body called the *crop,* or *honey stomach.* This stomach is separate from her other stomach. As she goes from flower to flower she comes in contact with a yellow powder called *pollen.* Some of the pollen is collected in little "baskets" formed by the special hairs on her hind legs.

As the forager bee collects nectar, she carries pollen from flower to flower. This is part of a process called *pollination*. When she has visited many flowers and her crop is full, she "beelines" back to her hive.

POLLINATION is the movement of pollen from the stamen to the stigma of the same kind of plant. This makes seeds to grow new plants.

STIGMA

STAMEN

POLLEN

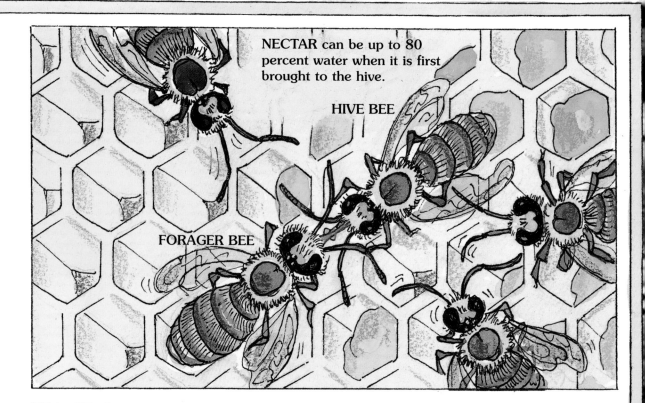

HONEY CELL

NECTAR can be up to 80 percent water when it is first brought to the hive.

HIVE BEE

FORAGER BEE

WAX-MAKING BEE

Back inside the hive the forager bee brings up, or regurgitates, the nectar. Then she transfers it by tongue to a hive bee. The nectar is passed by tongue among the hive bees until some of its moisture is gone. Then a wax-making bee places the nectar in a honey cell. There it continues to dry.

HONEY is about 18 percent water.

More and more nectar is added to the honey cell. House bees cluster over the cell and fan their wings to evaporate even more of the moisture in the nectar. As the nectar loses water, it becomes thicker and thicker. Finally, wax-making bees cap, or seal, the cell with wax. Slowly the nectar ripens into honey.

DANCES OF THE......

THE CIRCLE DANCE

The forager honeybee circles in one direction, turns around, and circles back the other way. This dance tells the other forager bees to look for new flowers anywhere within 300 feet of their hive.

When forager bees return to their hive they have a special way of telling the other forager bees of important discoveries... like a new location of flowers full of nectar and pollen. They do the dances of the bees.

HONEYBEES

A forager honeybee can visit up to 10,000 flowers a day. All the nectar she collects in her entire life can make only about one teaspoon of honey. To make one pound of honey, it takes nectar from over one million flowers. Also, different kinds of honey come from different kinds of flowers.

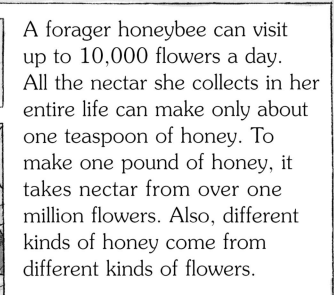

THE WAG-TAIL DANCE

This dance tells the other forager honeybees that the flowers are farther than 300 feet away. The direction she dances while wagging her tail tells where the flowers are in relation to the sun. The number of wags per 15 seconds tells how far away the flowers are.

WILD HIVE

HOLLOW LOG HIVE

CLAY POT HIVE

SKEP

HANGING MOVABLE-FRAME BEEHIVE

Honeybees have always been valued for the honey they make. For thousands of years, people have stolen honey from wild beehives. People became beekeepers when they began to make their own hives. Some used hollow logs. Others used clay pots. Later, in about 1500, European beekeepers started using upside-down basket hives called *skeps*. Then, in about 1850, the *hanging movable-frame beehive* was invented.

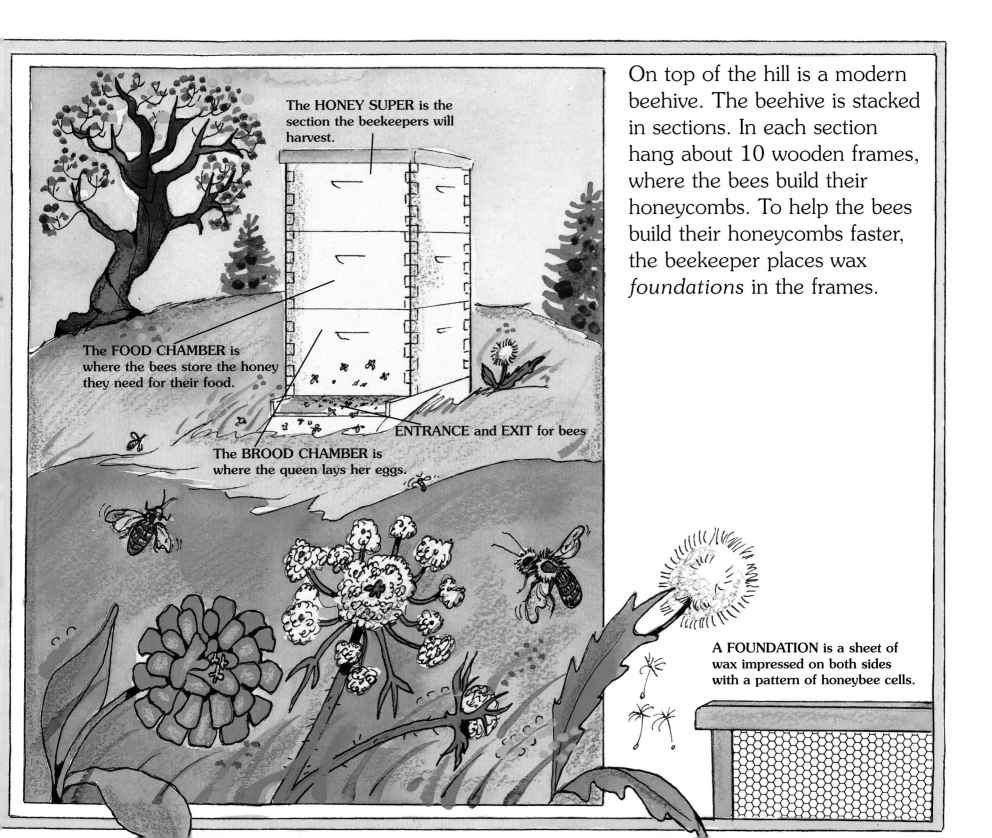

The HONEY SUPER is the section the beekeepers will harvest.

The FOOD CHAMBER is where the bees store the honey they need for their food.

The BROOD CHAMBER is where the queen lays her eggs.

ENTRANCE and EXIT for bees

On top of the hill is a modern beehive. The beehive is stacked in sections. In each section hang about 10 wooden frames, where the bees build their honeycombs. To help the bees build their honeycombs faster, the beekeeper places wax *foundations* in the frames.

A FOUNDATION is a sheet of wax impressed on both sides with a pattern of honeybee cells.

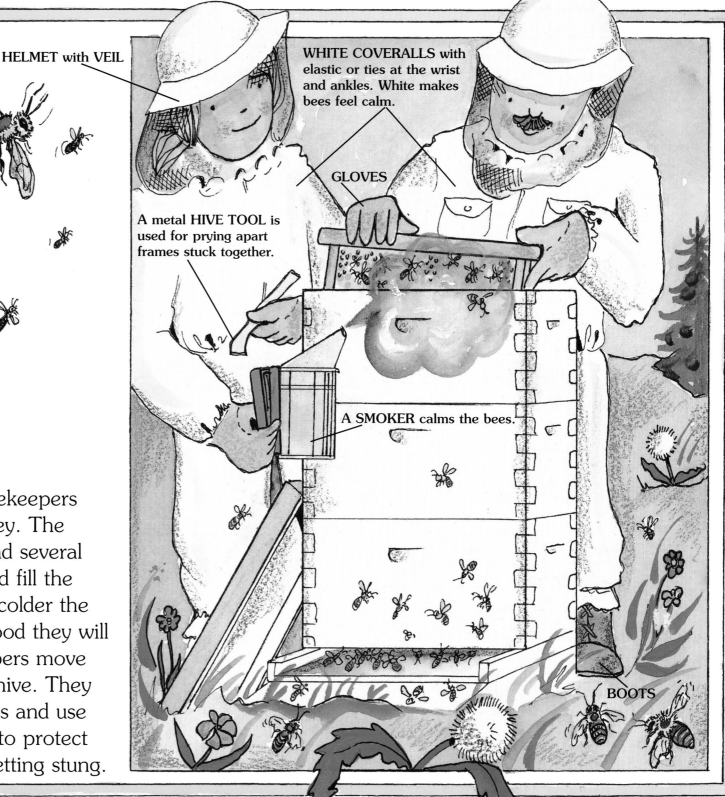

HELMET with VEIL

WHITE COVERALLS with elastic or ties at the wrist and ankles. White makes bees feel calm.

GLOVES

A metal HIVE TOOL is used for prying apart frames stuck together.

A SMOKER calms the bees.

BOOTS

It's time for the beekeepers to harvest the honey. The honeybees have had several months to build and fill the honeycombs. The colder the winter, the more food they will need. The beekeepers move slowly around the hive. They wear special clothes and use special equipment to protect themselves from getting stung.

KNIFE

EXTRACTOR

COLLECTING
TANK

Back at home, in a shed, the beekeepers use a hot knife to cut the wax caps off the honeycomb. Then the honeycomb frame is placed inside an *extractor*. It spins around at a high speed to remove the honey without breaking the honeycomb. The honey goes into a *collecting tank*.

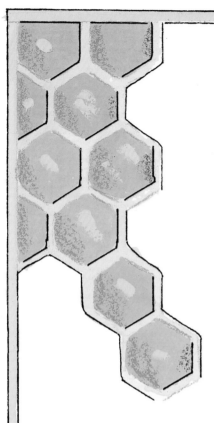

Next, the honey is filtered through a screen and a cloth to remove small pieces of wax. Then the honey is packed in airtight jars. Sometimes beekeepers melt down old and damaged honeycombs to make beeswax candles and other things. The rest of the empty honeycomb frames are returned to the hive for the honeybees to fill again.

For some beekeepers, honey making is a hobby. They use the honey themselves or give it away as gifts. Commercial beekeepers provide stores and shops with gleaming jars of their product to sell...delicious sweet honey from the honey makers.

A BEEKEEPER'S YEARBOOK

JANUARY

It's been really cold! All was safe at the hive after a blowing storm. The bees stay clustered around their queen to stay warm, rotating from the outside to the inside of the cluster, where it is about 95°F.

FEBRUARY

Still cold. We inspected the hive to see if the bees have enough honey left. All is well. The queen is beginning to lay eggs for the new honey-making season.

MARCH

Spring is coming. We uncovered the hive and inspected the bees again. Some days it gets up to 54°F, and a few bees are out looking for nectar.

APRIL

Another inspection. The worker bees are becoming more active. We see them hurrying to and from the hive. They're collecting nectar from early spring blossoms.

MAY

Lots of activity at the hive now that many spring flowers are in bloom. The hive must have become too crowded, because the old queen left in a swarm with about half the colony. The new queen looks healthy, so we won't have to replace her.

JUNE

The bees have been "busy as bees." They have been zooming to and from the hive, collecting nectar from early summer flowers. We inspected the bees and added another super.

JULY

We collected honey from the top super, then replaced it. The frames were full of honey. Later we had to stack on another super because the bees are producing so much.

AUGUST

Activity continues. Some workers are already getting ready for winter. They are patching cracks inside the hive with propolis to keep the cold winter air out. We gathered more honey. Fewer eggs are being laid.

PROPOLIS is a glue that bees make from plant resins.

SEPTEMBER

Activity at the hive is slowing down. The bees are still collecting nectar from fall flowers. We noticed the drone bees were being pushed out of the hive to die. This way the workers and the queen will have more honey for themselves.

OCTOBER

It's quiet around the hive. The food chamber is full of enough honey to get the colony through the winter.

NOVEMBER

We went up the hill to wrap the hive to help keep it warm inside. At this time of year the queen doesn't lay any more eggs. That way the colony won't grow too large for its food supply.

DECEMBER

What a cold winter. We know the bees are keeping warm inside their hive by clustering together. They have lots of honey to live on, up to 40 to 60 pounds per hive. We gave beautiful jars of honey and beeswax candles as gifts for Christmas this year.

HUMMM...

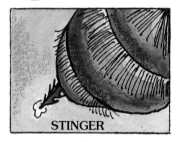

STINGER

WARNING! Worker bees can give painful stings. When a honeybee stings, tiny hooks, called *barbs,* on the stinger keep it from coming out of the victim's skin. The stinger has poison on it. When the bee flies away, the stinger stays behind. The bee dies, because its insides are damaged. So bees sting only when they or their hive is in danger.

Some people are allergic to bee stings and, if stung, can become very sick or die. Never approach a hive in the wild or a commercial hive unless you're with beekeepers and you're dressed for protection. If you get stung, tell an adult right away.

About 8,000 years ago, Greeks used the honeybee as a design on coins.

Individual beekeepers prefer different strains of honeybees. Some common strains are Italians, Germans, Carnolians, and Caucasians, as well as the African honeybees.

Swarming happens when the old queen and some of the colony leave to find a new home—when a hive becomes overcrowded or a new queen takes over. The new queen will sting any other queen bee's brood cells. This kills any developing queens, ensuring that she remains the only one. Unlike the stingers of worker bees, the queen's stinger does not come out of her body.

The cells of a honeycomb tilt slightly upward so the honey won't spill out.

On a hot summer day, the worker bees keep the hive cool inside by fanning their wings.

There are about 8,000 cells in each honeycomb frame.

Apiculture is beekeeping or the study of honeybees.
An *apiary* is a beeyard, or place where colonies of bees are kept.

Honeybees pollinate more flowers than any other insect. Some commercial beekeepers provide pollination services for agriculture.

CLOVER HONEY

Bees make different flavors and shades of honey. That's because they collect nectar from different kinds of flowers.

BUCKWHEAT HONEY

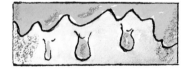

Some colonies can produce 500 pounds of honey in a year.

Throughout the world beekeepers harvest about one million tons of honey each year. The United States ranks third in the world in honey production.